The Immolation

The Immolation

Poems by

Douglas James Martin

Darkness Visible Books

La Jolla 2009

First edition published in 2009 by

Darkness Visible Books
P.O. Box 577
La Jolla, CA 92038
darknessvisiblebooks@yahoo.com

Copyright © 2009 by Douglas James Martin

All rights reserved. No part of this book may be used or reproduced in any matter whatsoever without written permission, except in the case of brief quotations embodied in critical articles or reviews.

Some of the poems which appear in this collection previously appeared in the following publications:

Kickass Review: "Aubade," "I Put my Hand in the Stream," "Cedar Fire," "La Jolla Christmas," "Today the Sun;" *Big Bridge:* "Manifesto of the Novanaive;" *San Diego Poetry Annual:* "Marriage Like War;" *Welcome, Eavesdropper:* "Hearts of Air."

All phrases in the poem "Slicing the Source" were taken from *Inside Microsoft SQL Server 7.0,* by Kalen Delaney.

Many thanks to Anna Zappoli Jenkins for the illustrations to "Four Emblems," on pages 52–55, to Dan Adams for the illustrations to "A Muddled Journey" on pages 30–32, and to Gabriela Anaya Valdepeña for the photograph on page 163. All other illustrations in "A Muddled Journey" are by the author.

Cover artwork from a painting by Anna Zappoli Jenkins.

FIRST EDITION

Printed in the United States of America

Library of Congress Control Number: 2009940325

ISBN: 978-0-9774000-4-1

For Gabriela

CONTENTS

AFTER THE FACT

Night and Daylight	3
Nothing but the Silence	4
Warts and All	5
A Breeze Upon the Lake of Fire	6
The Fancy's Subtlest Enemy	7
Now Jackie Lounges	8
How Do We Play the Scholar's Game?	9
Upon a Pool of Bile and Blood	10
The Divine Voluptuary	11
My Love Stepped Out	12
Do They Belong?	13
A Neighbor's Child	14
A Senseless Stone	15
Lucky Homer	16
Timothy Gerbil	18
That Woman	19
Midway to My Office	20
This Is for You	22

A MUDDLED JOURNEY

Canto One	25
Canto Two	29
Canto Three	36

POETRY IS A LIE

Envoi	45
Poetry Is a Lie	46
To My Wife	47
On Our Parents' 50th	48
Your Art	49
The Texan's Farewell	50
His Ribs Speak	51
Four Emblems	52
An Apology	56
Remade	57
Blues for Russel	58
La Jolla Christmas	60
Forgive, Kristine	62
Again, Last Night	63
Slicing the Source	64
From a Lost Play	65
I Put My Hand in the Stream	66
Today the Sun	68

MAGNETIC

Beneath the Black Parting	71
A Languid, Delicate Sausage	71
Men Are but an Ache	71
What Chant?	72
From the Cool Apparatus	72

Winter Dreams	72
After Frantic . . .	73
Under a Raw Moon	73
Eternity Is Rusting	73
A Tiny Puppy Tongue	74
He Is Watching	74
Why Did My Elaborate Lie?	74
Do Not Leave Me, Love	75
A Man of Womanly Likeness	75
So He Asked	75
Here	76

RANDOM WORDS

The Gigolo's Lament	79
The Vow	80
Shall I Wax Choleric	81
You Trouble My Dreams	82
The Lanai	83
The New Symposium	84
The Altruist	85
The Heart's Rough Traces	86
My Disillusion	87
The Scent of You	88
Ordinary Joy	89
To Science Wed	90

SONGS WITHOUT EARS

Heraclitus the Dark	93
Good	96
It's a Mystery	98
Talking to Tomorrow	100
The Boston Company Anthem	102
The Investment Manager's Promise	104
Johnny and Sue	105
The Derivatives of Love	106
Texas Wind	108
Trip West	111
Kristine	112
Greenhead	114
Pannikin	116
Burn On	118
Turnaround	120
Cold	122
She's So Sad	124
Not Afraid	126
I Didn't Do Nothing	128
Keith Wanted	130
Sixty Years	132
I Wished Her Dead	134

THE IMMOLATION

When I See the Lark	139
I Wish My Arms	142
The Sky Asked	143
Aubade	144
Anabelly Blues	145
Cedar Fire	146
Winter Solstice	147
The Little White Dog	148
Redondillas	149
Legitimate Form	152
Madrigal	153
Hearts of Air	154
Marriage, Like War	155
The Conqueror	156
We Can't Help It	157
To My Father	158
The Passions of Jacques Batârd	160

MANIFESTO OF THE NOVANAIVE

Homer Went Blind	169
Thee Fancies	170
A Thicket of Aphorisms	172
What We Need Now!	174

After the Fact

*Out of the first pleasures of the senses,
sown upon the bleak earth:*

Night and daylight merging,
paddles splash
in water, strangely changing:
midnight warmth
to midday cool.

Night, and daylight merging,
swift canoe
through atmospheres transforming:
chill of dark
to mild day.

An eerie mist is rising,
cry of loon
resounds, slowly dying,
shrill at first,
echoes soon.

The eerie mist dispersing,
beating sun
renounces cool morning:
a foggy birth,
a fire by noon.

Into the blank chill of the Ontario night he breathes his simple passions:

Nothing but the silence of the sky,
the distant, icy stars flashing,
a chill wind upon my face,
and echoing footsteps from the street
resounding in the frozen air.

Nothing but the music of the night,
the stars behind the clouds, peeking,
dancing snow upon my face,
laughing footsteps, light and free,
rejoicing in the joyful white.

Nothing but the fury of the wind,
the blackened, frenzied sky, writhing,
icy blasts against my face,
labored steps through driving snow
resisting the rebellious air.

Nothing but a stillness on the earth,
the silent smothered fields, gleaming,
gentle breezes on my face,
steady steps though squeaking snow:
muffled music in the frozen night.

An innocent cynicism bears its first affected fruit:

Warts and all, a squatting Cromwell,
hinds and forelegs poised to jump
from the common lily leaves, eyes
the royal pad

of Charles the toad, who huffs and puffs
through a folded beard of bloated skin.
An army, about, keeps common out
and noble in.

But the people, let by warts and all,
cut through the lines,
and the king is pushed from the royal pad
into the swim,
and a thousand warts now squat upon
the severed head,

and Cromwell covets the lily the king lay in.

Haunted by stern images of ancestral pioneers, he rails in dramatic verse against the unsatisfied dead:

A breeze upon the lake of fire;
the earth is simmering,
charred, and cracked;
gas escapes and dances, shimmering
in the glow of the flames.
A furnace,
a prison for my soul.

A breeze upon the lake of fire.
The earth itself is shivering,
frozen and cracked;
a mist escapes and dances, quivering
in the ice of the flames.
A furnace,
a prison for my soul.

He dreams. He hesitates:

The Fancy's subtlest enemy is fear,
the cancer that infects the infant dream,
rents the brain's fibers, and chokes the spirit
yearning to breathe into the withered frame

of the dying world. Here lies the body: comatose,
while groping, shaking hands, unskilled, unsure,
molest the flesh, feel for conspicuous tears
that might be sutured with a signature.

And now the clay arises! Shivers rend
the spine straight, while cold limbs feel the quick
passion of rushing blood; the cracked lips open;
the creature breathes, it seems about to speak . . .

But now a final shudder; all is still
And hollow as the surgeon's shrunken will.

Is she lost to him, that warm girl from Winnipeg?
In the cracked glass of desire she appears as a bored
courtesan, unwilling exile from a cold capital:

Now Jackie lounges on the stuffed divan,
a Marlborough dangling loosely from her lip,
and now and then, with a subtle turn of hand,
she shakes a somber rain from the glowing tip.

It's dark, and silent, that is if one forgets
The TV's faint reflection on the sash,
and chooses, rather, to watch that cigarette
grow cold beneath a thickening layer of ash.

She yawns, at last, and pulls a fresh one out,
reclines, inhales; the tip grows bright and clear;
her lips embrace it with a rounded pout;
she turns and whispers in my erect ear:

"Butt this for me, won't you, on your way out?
It's late, and time for me to go to bed."

A worm disturbs the sleeping host:

How do we play the scholar's game?
We dig up the dead and mock their breath,
then penetrate them with our schemes,
like worms, and thus assure their death.

What is the scholar's fervent aim?
Blood for old ghosts. The veil of death
is penetrated with new dreams;
this coupling will lend them breath.

With a Cartesian disinterest he chants the cruelty of art:

Upon a pool of bile and blood
the brain floats in the bowels,
soaking the sleeping spirits up
like a crumpled paper towel.

Trailing nets of capillaries,
it drags the draining ocean,
straining through the sluiceward streams
for the dregs of dormant notions,

'til treasures from the slurious deep,
lie shining and ambrosial,
and, like a filthy sponge, the brain
slips down the disposal.

*So, too, in the visions of Pythagoras, the one
and the many wrestle in a sad embrace:*

The divine voluptuary,
alone in the dark and empty womb,
bursts his heavenly passion
with a rush of heat into the cold.

Let us sing praises to our own
unfallen Onan.
Give praise to God, who with ungrudging goodness
spilt his seed into the void.

He is released from the bitter courses of love:

My love stepped out, one winter,
to piss into the cold
a ring of liquid fire
she couldn't hold.

She warned me that this liquor
would poison when old;
so when the wine turned bitter
she flushed me out, in gold.

Purging both lust for the daughter and respect for the father, he lacerates, according to rite, the sacrificial bourgeois:

Do they belong upon this muddled earth? —
those clean-limbed, perfect daughters,
with their good wishes, their well-meaning smiles,
the heavenly vacancy of their minds
unburdened by the sad heaviness of the flesh.
Their fathers have worked long hours, in tedious sacrifice
to the future, to these perfect children, who one and all
shall marry doctors, lawyers, young executives,
and flit their lives away in perfect happiness.
How sad shall heaven seem
to those who have never dreamed earth's bitter dream.

He measures the homely blessings of majority:

A neighbor's child was careless in her play.
She rushed into the busy street, where
indifferent wheels released
her white brains to the black asphalt.

Our eager, urgent paperboy,
lost in some furious adolescent vision,
could never turn to worldly things again. He found
consummation in his father's rifle.

Our minister's daughter fancied herself fit
for sacrifice, in the name of reform.
She married an ex-con, who
beat her to death, after a few weeks.

I, too, have unrequited dreams,
and some remains of stubborn, stupid youth,
though, blessed with a little homely prudence,
I will take my time.

*He imagines himself as a marble Priapus, lending
a cold pleasure to the adoring Bacchae:*

"My love," she cried, "are you a senseless stone?
Will your lips never yield to sighing fears?
Will your eyes never flood with nervous tears?
Will you stand, forever, silent and alone?

"The strand has never seen my name inscribed;
nor have my praises graced the turning day.
Why must the cliff disdain the yielding clay
and mock the changes of the wind and tide?

"My love," she cried, "I beg you to decide:
shall this poor, naked, crumbling earth be whole,
stamped with the emblem of your diamond soul?"
But pitiless as an oracle, he replied:

"Love traced in dust, in a day, shall be erased.
Love carved in stone will never be effaced."

He flees with a traveling band, proclaiming his dying song before the ignorant ears of barbarian children:

Lucky Homer, naked on the beach,
he stares at the naked sun with naked
eyes, burning, alive with pain.
That one undying vision still
remains.

Alone at the beach I stare at the fading
sun, hoping to discover something
new, that cannot pass away
beneath the shade
of my dark glasses.

She asked me: "How can you cry at a movie?
I never heard you cry for me!" Well I don't
know why I'm always so sentimental;
what I really want
is to be naïve.

She asked me: "Why, when you tell me that you love me,
You say it with a smile?" Well I said:
"You can have my body, but my
soul won't be stripped
of it's irony."

Do you hear the sound of the siren singing
a song about a song about
seduction, by obscurity?

Resistance melts.
My voice withers.

Listen to you listen to me listen to the past
listen to a dying muse sing a dying
song. Can you catch the cry of the word—
naked, and dying
of exposure?

He mourns the death of a favorite pet:

Stiff like cardboard, stretched on the floor we found him.
Cardboard lingered, unchewed, in his silent cage. Now
cold he lies, all alone, in a cardboard coffin—
Timothy Gerbil.

Bright he was, far brighter than all the others.
Quickly he learned his pace on the plastic play disc,
sweetest too, so gentle his disposition.
Why did he leave us?

June-chan, Douglas, and Alfie prepared the gravesite;
Mel and Mad Max sent flowers, and Fatso seedlings;
Maua sent lettuce, Warrior and Danger shavings;
Runt sung the dirges.

Then we left him. Down by the Charles he lies. Though
now, perhaps, his teeth, without wood to wear them,
nourished by river water, will grow, like an ivory
ladder, towards heaven.

*What black root will charm this mistress? She
alone can guide him, whole, through the school
of the silent dead:*

That woman baffles me. Why can't we all
aspire to speak plainly? In plain words, easily
satisfied, modest words that say what they mean
and then retire decently, like the discarded
paperwork from a problem set—it stays in the bin!

But this witch won't allow that. No!
I seize my pen, but she's always taking over!
My eyes smear, my limbs writhe like
snakes loose in hot sand, my body pierced
by a thousand of my own unexpected
erections, her round belly gaping
like the grave, while her sweet, caressing arm,
like a golden noose, yanks my head into the sky.

Nothing will knit. Nothing will stay in its place.
Old Ez knew it; in the end one remains silent.

*His music fled, his metaphysics cold, he waits upon
the vacant echoes of autumn:*

Midway to my office, late, one autumn morning,
on the winding path by the Charles' scruffy bank,
I pause for a moment, while the year turns upside down.

Where are they now, the bright, stubborn blossoms
that I still remember from an early spring?
The empty branches twist, like exposed roots,
naked in the cold air of vacant November;
and even the fallen leaves have vanished, swept
by an anxious wind to warm decay. Only
their scattered signs, black on the grey pavement,
linger, in the silence, like nostalgic ghosts.

Was there a prophecy written on these leaves
before they received their definitive translation?
As a child I loved to gaze at the yellowing pages
of an old paperback from my father's library:
"A Pictorial History of the Third Reich;" and there,
amongst portraits of naked women before the gas chambers,
and grim landscapes of blasted baroque cities,
were some fine silhouettes of Japanese gentleman and ladies,
charred in carbon against a concrete abutment,
with the aid of a very hot flash; but now the sun
lies low and cold, like the bulb in a large freezer,
and I wait, a live shade in a fading picture.

Could this be where it was leading—that beautiful, boundless
thought, that stubborn dreaming? Somewhere, someone

has died; I have missed the funeral; and now I am haunted
by a time when time seemed endless, a time now ended,
by a proud certainty, shrunk into isolation,
by a foolish hope, stiffened into paralysis;
so I wait for a great light, midway on a walk to my office.

A sadder man, he returns, with a new hope, to his first muse:

This is for you, who were kind to me,
at the precipice of my puberty,
for the science fiction we'd consume
on long, Ottawa afternoons,
for freckles, and precocious breasts
in your pink, prudish, bathing dress,
for trembling legs, and your wet hair,
when I kissed you shyly, on a dare,
and the clumsy way that we caressed
in the pool, by the officer's mess,

and last, for your forgiveness, when
I turned, foolishly, in the end,
to the skinny girl in the green bikini;
I know, now, you were best for me,
and I still remember how you stood
crying, when I left town for good.

Perhaps I shouldn't be turning back,
twenty years after the fact,
to memories so shamefully full
of sentiments so trivial,
but now that my youth is almost through
I feel I must give homage to
you, who were there when it all began,
So please forgive me, if you can;
accept, despite the deferred fashion,
this gift of a long belated passion.

The Muddled Journey

CANTO ONE

ARGUMENT— His PhD abandoned, Douglas is forced to find a job. After taking the Red Line from Cambridge, he ascends from the Boston Common subway station, then struggles up Beacon Hill towards an imposing office tower on its crest. There he hopes to become an editor in the trade division of an old and prestigious publishing firm. Midway up the hill, pain from the torn meniscus in his right knee frustrates his progress, and his spirit, until the ghost of Henry Houghton, drifting towards him from the Granary Burying Ground, offers to be his comrade and his guide.

Midway in the muddled journey of my life
    I found myself near the base of a dark tower,
    bowed down with sorrow at the endless strife

that led me, stumbling, to my bleakest hour,
    when fear and fate, at once, conspired to rob
    the quiet pleasure of my ivory bower,

thrusting me straight amongst the desperate mob
    of souls, defeated, yet desiring still,
    now prowling Limbo begging for a job.

With a long sigh I mounted the gloomy hill
    o'er which that tower gloated, a beacon black
    beckoning all whose pale, exhausted will

the frets of bitter resignation wrack,
    and through the morning mist groped for the trail,
    'til my legs faltered at an awesome crack

yawning, it seemed, within myself—the bale
    of carelessness, and stubborn vanity,
    when leaping from the bed this aging male

ripped the cartilage in his weakening knee—
    and now a surfeit of meniscal strain
    mocked e'en my shrunken hopes with misery

while wasted years tolled with a ringing pain.
    Thus blank at heart, I hobbled down the slope,
    all confidence abandoning, again,

and would have withered with my blasted hope
    had not a hoarse disturbance reached my ear,
    as if a swinging corpse, e'en from the rope,

whispered a final pleading. Looking near
    for the cryptic source of that uncanny sound
    my eyes alighted on a mouldy bier.

There in the midst of an ancient burial ground,
    at the crumbling base of some dull monument
    an ectoplasmic mist was gathering 'round,

which soon resolved itself into the spent
    form of a man, or former man, and spake:
    "My name was Henry Houghton, beneficent

"patron of all who think, and all who make
    out of air and ink immortal memories
    (and all who peddle these words for profit's sake!)

"Lucky for you I happed this morn to please
    my restless ghost visiting Paul Revere
    or I might ne'er have had the chance to ease

"your body's frailty and your spirit's fear—
    Arise my friend! Stiffen your will to steal
    the day's promise, for I shall linger here,

"a steady comrade, and a sturdy keel,
    firming your errant soul to the deadly climb,
    prodding your drooping virtue. Waken! Heal!

Erect a palace from the ruins of time!"
    With that he gently grasped my willing arm,
    and led me, gingerly, 'mongst cliffs sublime

dwarving our petty forms; yet no alarm
    hectored my balance, or disturbed my path,
    secure, it seemed, from horror and from harm.

The comforts of the dead, however, hath
    limited warmth before a living wind;
    and often does Dame Fortune's furious wrath

the hasty promises of hope rescind—
    So thought I as I reached that tower's base
    where fattened fantasies were cruelly thinned

by the desperate sheerness of its brooding face.

CANTO TWO

ARGUMENT— Douglas, led by the ghost of Henry Houghton, arrives at the base of the tower at One Beacon Street. They pause to note the fearsome legend hung over the corporate exercise club, then slip artfully past the security guard toward the central bank of elevators. During the long ascent towards Human Resources on the 26th floor, Henry reveals to Douglas a vision west across the Charles river, where the new Software Division building gleams in the early morning sun. Within, sundry linguists and coders labor together on the next edition of their famous dictionary.

    THROUGH ME THE PLACE WHERE FRAZZLED SINEWS KNIT.
        THROUGH ME THE DREAD MACHINES OF CARNAL GRACE.
        THROUGH ME THE WEAK STIFFEN TO CORPSES FIT

    FOR OVERTIME, WITHOUT COMPLAINT, OR PAY,
        AND SMILES ETERNAL, E'EN AS THROATS ARE SLIT—
        ABANDON ALL EASE, YE MORTALS DOOMED TO STAY.

So read the legend on that awful gate
    barring the sinister end of a vast bay
    wherein a ghostly rabble did await

the grudging favor of a frowning guard,
    whose rigid niceties would soon frustrate
    the savviest sailor or the wiliest bard.

"Hold!" he howled, "Who can ye be who dare
    to breach the tower walls without that card
    grudging you license to this evil lair?"

At that my guide girded each ghostly loin,
    and answered vacant look with vitreous stare:
        "Officious fool," he mocked in fierce rejoin,

"do you not know me? Have you no respect
    for substance purer than the paltry coin
        vouched by the gods to whom you genuflect?"

Next, my friend to the floor contemptuously cast
    some sullied gold, and, like a loath insect,
        the guard grubbed in the dust as we slithered past.

As the numberless leaves of late October clog
    November's burdened drains, while with'ring blasts
    from eager winter press them to a bog,

so now did anxious spirits crowd the hall,
    while false drafts of anticipation flogged
    our piteous forms towards a puny stall

where elevating engines 'gan to run,
    and my enervated mind did further pall,
    seeing the dole so many had undone.

"Be comforted," dear Henry now consoled,
    "E'en in the closest vice of hell, the sun
    a sweet effulgence sheds on those who hold

"fast to the efflorescence of their guide."
>Then, with a sweep of phantom arm he rolled
>backwards the roiling shades on either side,

until one wall of the rising car was clear
>of all obstruction, and upon this wide
>screen a resplendent vision did appear—

I saw a river, broad and flecked with sail,
>full with the promise of that vast frontier
>flooding boundlessly west, where never pale

prudence can dam the bed of lusty thought,
>   where every seed that fancy might conceive
>   on an ever big futurity is begot.

Beyond that stream—though I could scarce believe
>   the wonder that the architect had wrought—
>   a palace of pink stone did proudly cleave

the wanton Sky, who amorously sought
>   in turn to have the beauty of its eye
>   in high facades of emerald mirrors caught.

Within—for wondrously far could I espy—
>   masterful sages paced their learned cells,
>   the keeps of language dreaming to defy

with the sly keys of their electric spells,
>   (rememb'ring, too, how metaphysical ware
>   yet shines with solid lustre when it sells!)

There one might labor long without despair
>   and breed a swelling notoriety,
>   amazing lesser wits with talent rare

For wedding ancient Greek to modern C!
>   But ere my bucking fantasies could bolt
>   the chafing stalls of niggard reality,

the elevator halted, with a jolt.

34	CEO	SATAN
33	V.P.'s	TREASON
32	TRADE	FRAUD
31	REFERENCE	VIOLENCE
30	CORRELATIONS	HERESY
29	SCHOOL MATH	WRATH
28	SCHOOL ENGLISH	AVARICE
27	COLLEGE DIVISION	GLUTTONY
26	HUMAN RESOURCES	LUST
ELEVATOR	VISION OF SOFTWARE DIVISION	THE VIRTUOUS HEATHEN
LOBBY	GUARD	CHARON

ONE BEACON STREET

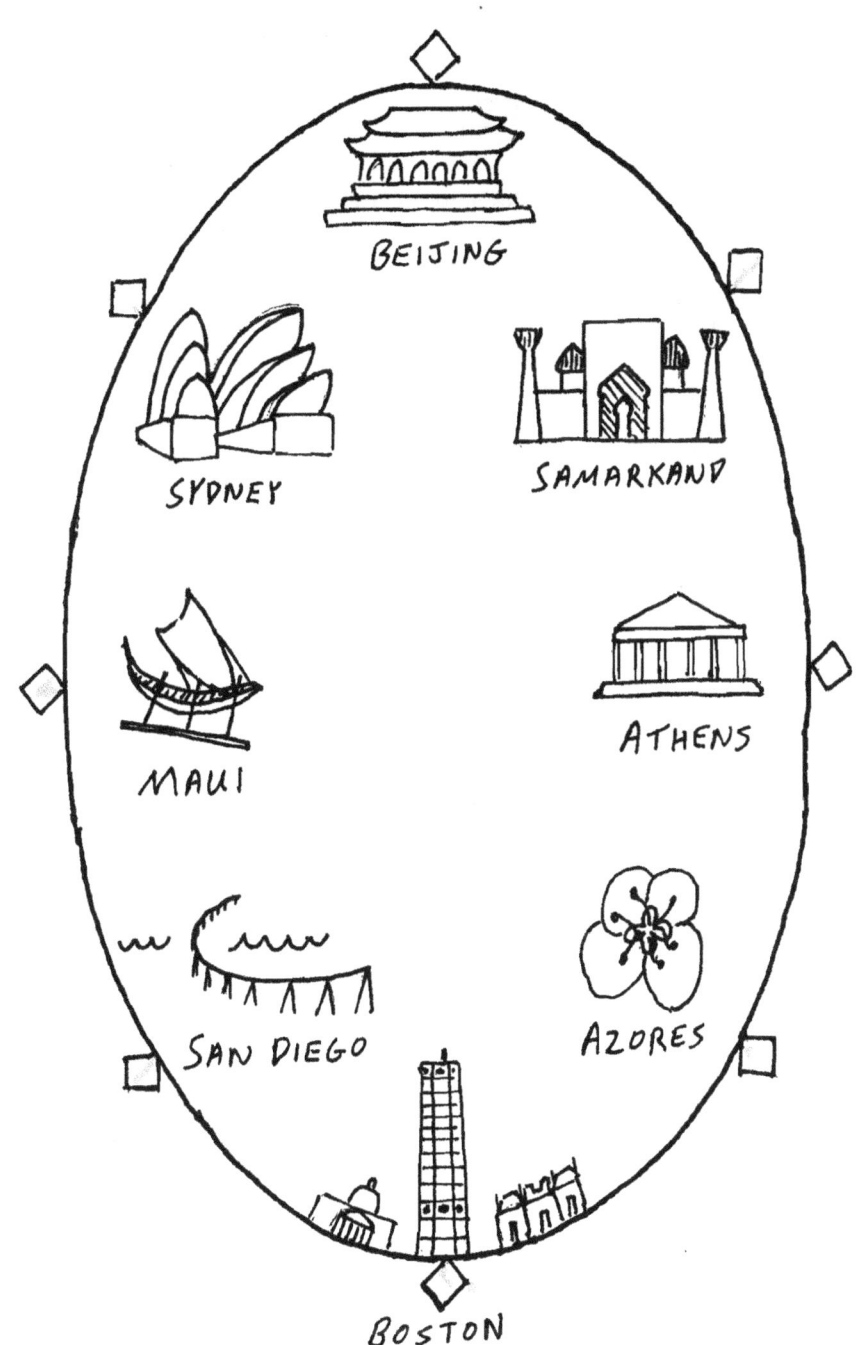

CANTO THREE

ARGUMENT— The elevator stops at Human Resources, where Douglas is forced out by a rush of spirits, and immediately buffeted by fearsome winds. Henry explains that the spirits haunting this floor are those perpetually tossed to and fro by unending dissatisfaction with their own careers. One of these spirits drifts close by, and can be heard, above the wind, chanting the joys and prospects of a pilgrimage to California, far from these gloomy Eastern skies. But the ghost soon slips away, whereupon Douglas finds himself seated before a lithesome siren of subtle and powerful charms. She sings to him sweetly of the many advantages, for the frustrated academic, of book editing, with its comfortable familiarity as well as its unexpected pleasures.

The doors slid open on floor twenty-six,
    just as a sudden gust of foul air
        expelled the ghosts in a thick phantasmal mix.

Like a starling coarsely tugged by its own snare
    I was tossed, helplessly, across the floor,
        first south, then east, towards I know not where,

until at last I lay, prostrate, before
    a polished desk, whose dainty limbs I held
        like a drown'd sailor embracing an alien shore.

Around me throngs of shrieking spirits welled
    forth from the whirling winds, and yet nearby
        my guide stood firm as oak, by storms unfelled.

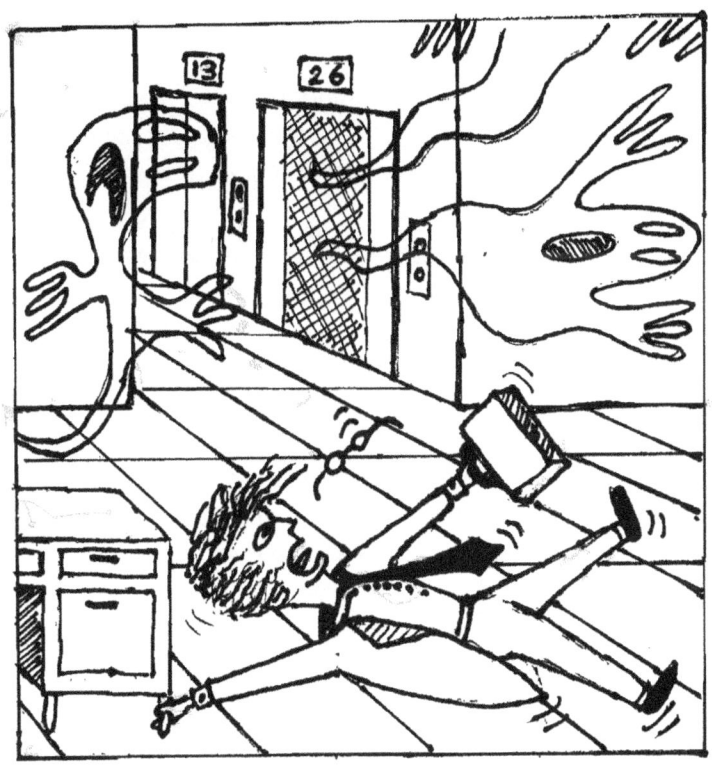

"What is this monarch realm?" 'gan I to cry,
    straining my voice against the tempest's rage.
    "Who are these shades dark'ning the raving sky?"

"This is a marketplace," replied my sage,
    "for rootless hopes, like yours, that e'er desire
    a larger, higher, and a richer cage.

"Like foolish moths, half-maddened by the fire,
    they flit from interview to interview,
    hot with delusions of a perfect hire."

"Surely," I answered, "this cannot be true
    of me?" but ere I mastered my own doubt
        a shade approached, declaiming as it flew—

> *In cruel Aprille, when showers with showers of soot*
> *contend in the burdened air, and underfoot,*
> *last autumn's rotting leaves remain to breed*
> *this summers' crop of roaches, rat, and weed,*
> *when fumes asphaltic, freed by sudden heat,*
> *inspire in every parking lot and street*
> *traffic jams, and the pimply sons of whores*
> *from pimping halls, turn pimping out of doors,*
> *and foul brats, with curses, taunts, and screams*
> *torture our sleep, and spoil our wettest dreams*
> *(so pricketh nature in our fallen hearts),*
> *than longen folk for trips to far-off parts;*
> *tourists, jobseekers, flush with bright green bills*
> *seek fresh delight, and unimagined thrills,*
> *and specially, from Maine to Idaho,*
> *to sunny California they go,*
> *its blissful sandy beaches for to seek*
> *that hem might mellow with a vague mystique.*

The song receded, though its echoes weak
    were answered still, in the corrosive lust
        those words had kindled in my burning cheek:

"What if I too should fly, and boldly thrust
    my feathered hope into the formless air,
        to passion willing all my passionate trust?

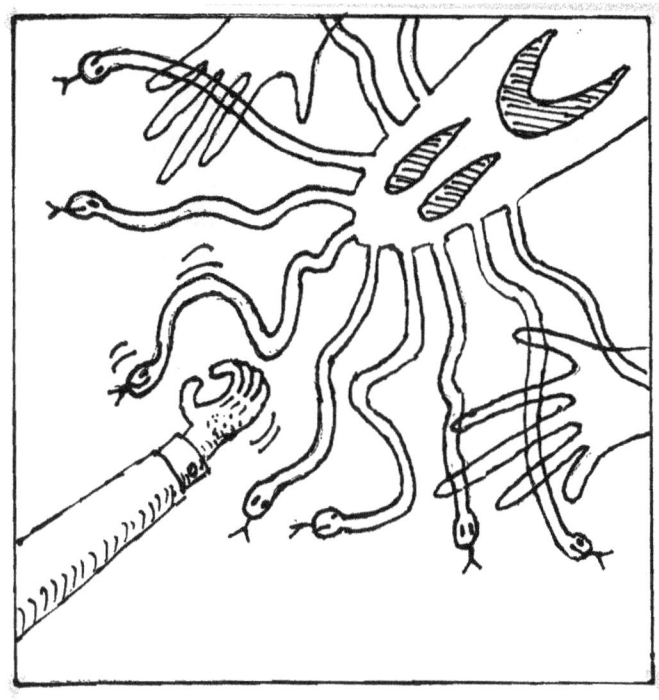

Or should I, rather, cradle in this lair,
    in the aging arms of a familiar coast?"
    In restless agony I seized the hair

that trailed in cloudy shadows from the ghost,
    hoping to force an answer from its sighs.
    But the icy tresses slipped, and the shade was lost.

Now, as a spritsail tortured by the skies
    yet grips the spar, I hung by fingertip,
    until a vision of resplendent thighs,

languid beneath the desk, strengthened my grip,
    much as the beauty of a figurehead
    heartens the mariner, and saves the ship.

"You will find harbor here, and friendship," said
    a honeyed voice, of such surprising force,
    saints would not scorn the shapely hand that led

to a sheltered chair, nor spurn her sweet discourse,
    which flooded my senses, and my common sense,
    with animal charm wed to inhuman resource:

"Yes, you may quibble with the trifling pence
    we call a wage, and yes, it would pacify
    only a trust-fund brat, but in our defense,

"we are a hermitage, the last standby
    for wand'ring scholars like you, whose fathers spawned
    faster than tenured faculty tend to die.

"Here you may nurture all the fancies fond
    that crowd, like tumors, your productive brain,
    without the bother of the deeper bond

"owed by a father to those thoughts that gain
    the freedom of the world. In fact we'll take
    that burden off you (though we shall retain

"full legal rights to them, for both our sake).
    And as you savor the fruits of our largesse
    at company dinners, familiar bread you'll break

"with many a famous poet, or poetess,
    whose talent, luck, or beauty might restore
    your own retreating fancies of success.

"And if they prove to be but pompous bores
	(which has been known to happen), please feel free
	to dazzle the interns with your trove of lore

"hoarded from Harvard days. I'm sure you'll see
	all 'round here many an egghead ingénue,
	who'll talk 'bout Chaucer, then—lend you her key."

With that I could no longer look into
	her amaretto eyes without a sob
	of resignation, wond'ring how she knew

that now I'd blush, and smile, and take the job.

Poetry is a Lie

Envoi

Go, little book, and let my meaning steal
betwixt these subtle bars of irony
into the unencumbered air, where all
our earth-vexed syllables can gather, free

as the swifts, twittering now in the summer dusk,
while tracing tiny orbits round the flue;
their intricate, willful retrogressions mock
the dumb rootedness of this hearth-fixed pole.

I cast the thrice burned *logos* on the fire,
and brace again to force my heart through my tongue.
The ancient rod stiffens again to flay
these words, this flesh, this breathing cage of bone.

Birds, and paper, fall at last to earth,
to rot, silently, 'til a careless breeze
tosses the ashes of their own desire
into the cold judgment of eternity.

Poetry Is a Lie

I am sick with Truth's sleepless, arrogant eye
stripping the living flesh from the living word.
Everyone knows that poetry is a lie.

Desire repents the power in his thigh,
and Beauty retreats, her reputation slurred,
shamèd by Truth's sleepless, arrogant eye.

Rhetoric lays the ancient drum aside,
while Music's primitive motives lie unheard.
Everyone knows that poetry is a lie.

Beneath this voice, a voiceless passion sighs,
cleaving to thought, not what you thought you heard,
hidden from Truth's sleepless, arrogant eye.

And though this silence issues in a sign,
that seed lives while sentence is deferred.
Everyone knows that poetry is a lie.

If my words offend thee, cut them free.
Then cast my body where my tongue's interred,
piercèd by truth's sleepless, arrogant eye.
Everyone knows that poetry is a lie.

To My Wife

Poets have long despaired the power to sing,
in hollow words, the fullness of their love.
I, too, can sense my language faltering
before the passion that your nature moves.

Philosophers say that passions often fail
before one thought's silent profundity.
Nor can my fleeting moods pretend to tell
what you have taught of love and ecstasy.

But the blankness of these failures cannot boast,
with a just force, the transcendence you have wrought,
nor speak the sweet disturbance that excites
my word, my blood, my vision, and my thought.

Could a speechless babe sing praises, as you bless,
with new waters, his newborn consciousness?

On Our Parents' 50th

Time has a way of turning all
prognostications risible,
while grudging, as our sinews slow,
a retrospective wisdom grow.
How else to explain this marriage, that
to children's eyes seemed nothing but
the simple background of our play,
a fact, as stable as the day,
something that helped our world seem
quite ordinarily serene?
But now that our eyes are wrinkling, too,
we might begin to give what's due.
We've felt the pain and bliss beneath
marriage's common countenance.
The cries of our own chaotic brood
now echo our noisy childhood.
We, too, have clenched bewildered fists
at life's absurd, malicious twists.
And now that we've seen the world straight,
this marriage, that once seemed nothing quite
remarkable, now stands revealed:
a miracle of fifty years.

One marriage, with the dew of love,
brought forth five branches into life.
Five married sons, in recompense,
now honor the root that gave them strength.
May we pass on, to our own kin,
our parents gift: a peace within
deeper even than memory —
a domesticated eternity.

Your Art

Now that your art has rushed upon its high career,
do not forget those common crafts, now left behind.
Someone must build the frame, and stretch the canvas taut,
before that blank suffers the visionary stain.

The Texan's Farewell

Forgive me, daughters, for rushing beyond
before you were ready to see me gone.
You know how I liked to come and go
with a brief good-bye, and a sudden hello.
How I loved to dodge the ruts of time,
tormenting the moon, and rousing the dawn.
Though now is a case, I must confess,
where my haste surprised even myself.

As for advice: would you trust from me
sage remarks on futurity?
But I knew how to make the moment last
in the heart, forever, before it passed.
So grab a few moments, while you're here
that you'll never tire of holding near.
And also, remember to tell your men—
I can whup them still, even where I am;
so they better take care of you girls well
or I'll haunt them into a Texas hell!

And as for my ashes, scatter them
on my favorite lake, in memoriam
of a place where my restlessness found peace,
in the heaven of a hunting lease.
There, my daughters, I'll rest fine,
while the crappies tug at every line,
while turkeys jostle to fill my sights,
and the deer battle to join the feast.
There, where even the possum's king
no man can want for anything.

His Ribs Speak

Dumb we are, and always obedient.
Our glassy sinews stretch to let escape
all promises, and at the least command
we yawn to charge the violent gasps, that spring
like conquering invaders, from your root.

Still, can another part proclaim as native this—
the soft impression of her cheek, at rest?

Four Emblems

At last the sullen spring bursts in a rush
of rude, green joy. Now hot youths scourge
the dumb flanks, and madden their steeds with haste,
while restless shoots trouble the wizened earth.

The mower sweats all morning, 'til the day's
zenith summons him to repose and rum.
There, like a patient general, he surveys
the hay fresh-cut, the haying yet to come.

Kind autumn, like a doting, elder kin,
the fruits of summer's labor freely shares,
'til ripeness seems exhausted, though within
the core runs golden, beneath branches bare.

Now January shrouds the empty fields
with silence, while the dim sun barely climbs
above the lowest mound, its modest wheel
reluctant to disturb the sleep of time.

An Apology

What can I bring to you, my wife,
worthy of your long sufferance,
to you—the center of my life—
uncentered by my thoughtlessness,
to you, the unexhausted spring,
greening the arid beds of care,
now clogged, as a muddy dullness brings
a decade's planning to despair?

Hope, perhaps, but this at least,
the one thing I am master of—
in ten short anniversaries,
ten thousand years of doting love.

Remade

Now, in my childish memories
                I hear your unmet voice,
and I wash the dishes drunk
                with your domestic logic;
now at my wrist I feel
                a pulse stronger than lust or anger.
Thus, love has remade me.

Blues for Russel

Brother:

When the sky's frieze cracks with lysergic fire,
        you hold us to the grid burned in the hills
                of San Francisco.
When the gods disembowel, soiling our mortal laps,
        you wash us in Bay waters, your smile
                disarming the irritated furies.
Where is that peace, now? Where is that stillness?

Old Friend:

When the Maui breeze, moist with sadness,
        clatters in the stiff, long leaves, you answer,
your touch quick to the sap
        coursing in sighs beneath the bark,
live to the voices hidden in the wood's deep chambers.

Comrade:

In the living streets I turn to share a joke,
        while throngs pass oblivious to our
                fraternal visions.
In a white room you pass me the lens,
        as the screen shakes with laughter, and
                the light freezes.
The exposure turns out blank, the meter zero.

New Friends:

When the music aches we ask you: "Who?"
        "I don't know!" you say, but are quick to
                raise the volume.
And the unknown voice rasps his particular pain,
        while you add punctuation on the conga.
Why do the dead sing bluer than the living?

Lover:

You hold me in your wiry arms,
        your body small, lithe, your breath gentle,
my body echoing yours,
        still smaller, lithe, languorous in your wiry
                           arms.
Where is that gentleness, whose echoes linger?

La Jolla Christmas

Here, where no one has ever seen
new snow cloaking an evergreen,
or revived with sweet hot chocolate
while fretting the frigging car to start,
where frostbitten cheeks will never know
warm lips beneath the mistletoe,
and the stars are deaf to the Glorias
ringing from frozen coils of brass,
the hapless natives do their best
nature's injuries to redress—
bereft of the gleam of Christmas skates
they rub roller-blades round dry lakes;
their feet unpressed in virgin snow
they pine for the morning mists to show;
while canyons ache for the cut of the sleigh
toboggans tumble along the waves;
and mirroring the supernal calm
bright garlands orbit the trunks of palms.

And yet, there is something suitable,
and more profoundly seasonal,
in this stripe of dreams and vanity
between the desert and the sea—
where bristling legions guard our doors
while angels shine on us from the north;
where still, like frightened shepherds, we cling
to the wheel of birth and suffering;
where seekers, too, of every age,
still hasten in joyful pilgrimage,

hoping to find another birth
in this ancient, yet engendering, earth,
while martyrs gleefully wrench these ties,
springing to spacecraft in the skies,
and madmen in the wilderness
sing to the stones their doleful cries.

So I, like every soul before,
am shipwrecked on this alien shore,
where love, and hope, and tenderness
lie drowned, while briny loneliness,
like scrapings from the Saltonsea
chastens the wounds enriving me,
and the California Aquaduct
can't slake the deserts in my heart.

Why was this world roughly made,
like a Quonset hut, in seven days,
with a floor of dirt, and a roof of tin
that scarcely keeps the warmth within?
Oh god, liar, myth, or man,
dear Christ, you saw this before you began.
As the stars fall down on Christmas morn,
grant me the courage to be born.

Forgive, Kristine

Forgive, Kristine, my boldness in
demanding, from your gentleness,
a muse's gaze empyrean,
and cold, tyrannical caress.

From you, who still live in paradise,
though blushing at your innocence,
and madly rushing to embrace
sad Eve's original recompense.

Will every maker, for his own,
seize the covenant of your thighs,
and build their monuments of stone
from the doomed softness of your eyes?

Again, Last Night

I dreamed of you again, last night. It had all
been decided: the old lover conveniently
usurped; your family now lined up like coral
gazing at a strange new fish. You stand, shyly,
between light and shadow, the noon sun tumbling
like surf on your black hair; your cheek, like polished
sandalwood, smooth against my own; your voice
breaking nervously as you begin the introductions.

Could this be real? I folded the faux lace
doily into the shape of a lance, and forced
the paper stiffly into my thumb.
                                        When I awoke
I was old again, remembering what had never been.

Slicing the Source

Without outside intervention,
            each program will wait forever.
Girls inner join boys;
            a parent row is deleted.
Rows without children,
            the highest level of isolation.
Triggers are a pollution;
            a system failure occurs!

It's critical to know
            which of the assertions was violated.
You try to delete Bob,
            which forces you to delete Betty.
Deleting an office
            causes deletion of the salespeople.
You can't change an office number;
            the Los Angeles office is deleted.

Economics was also a factor;
            consider again the chain of privileges.
A prohibition against transferring control,
            control over the flow of execution.
An infinite loop of fired triggers;
            you cannot drop the foreign key.
A vertical view slices the source.

From a Lost Play

Let me rut the vast cunt of the soulless world
and plug the ocean's drain with a heedless gasp,
until these haggard seas overwhelm the fields,
like a spent camp whore hobbling behind after
the towers have fallen, after the rapes are over,
to salt the crops.

I Put My Hand in the Stream

I put my hand in the stream,
through water cold to the wrist,
and wrenched a rock from its bed,
with a quick, sharp twist.

Scraping away the sand
and algae from its face,
I let the sunlight pierce
the smooth, crystalline flesh.

Nature had suffering right
long before our lessons began.
Its inarticulate pain
is written in weathered bones

of chicks expelled from the nest,
and weasels too old to mate,
who suffered, withered, and died
wordless, here on this bank.

Suffering poets, shut up!
If you can't carve your song
into something that gathers the light
I really don't give a damn.

Those who have yet to learn
won't understand your pain,
and those at the head of the class
don't need to hear it again.

So keep your tears to yourself.
Let them flow within, like a stream,
until they weather your heart
to a cold, bright stone.

Today the Sun

Today the sun cascades its endless youth
upon the promises you make, and all
is light. Freely you bind your wrists to truth
pledged in antiphon to the heart's call.

It's an ordinary San Diego day;
yet love has something more of Boston's stern
seasons in it: the spring can never stay
quite long enough, and summer sometimes burns
beyond its proper bound; the autumn may
be sad, though beautiful, and the bleak winter never turn.

Remember, then, the brightness of this time,
when the years bring on their legacy of pain.
Far from the innocent California sun
the depths of love can make all bright again.

Magnetic

1

Beneath the black part/ing
sweet gift/s live on:

Egg/s boil, white/ly.
Her iron moan/s.

But for death, she is near.

2

A languid, delicate sausage
shake/s the void.
Behind mist, smooth, easy
essential meat ask/s:
may I be
you/r repulsive love?

3

Men are but an ache
in life of girl.

Say: *no.*
Say: *a light blow, arm/ed*
with hot knife.

Delirious blood will sing.

4

What chant could incubate the moment?
A goddess' pink feet lather garden rain;
shadow/s crush with gorgeous day.

5

From the cool apparatus,
a thousand friend/s.
Flood/s of water/y vision drool
from my blue TV.

6

Winter dream/s of beauty
drive the lazy pole.
An enormous spring
heave/s bitter rock.

7

After frantic . . .
she felt lake wind
worship/ing he/r breast.
It is not sordid,
yet, a fiddle.

8

Under a raw moon
I sweat whisper/s.
Finger/ing her gown,
my language smear/d.

9

Eternity is rust/ing.
Forest & symphony
sag like hair & skin.
Though I storm/ed
like summer music,
I am about to fall.

10

A tiny puppy tongue,
wet and waxy as peach was red,
lick/ed playful/ly at our picture.

Next, it spray/ed in, on, at, & over
car, dress, and bed. In some urge/s

there is milky power.

11

He is watch/ing
when you show bare leg,
scream/ing
after you use up his juice.
He will pant, weak/ly,
think mad/ly,
and mother cry:
let him go!

12

Why did my elaborate lie
always soar above this road?
We smell sad, ugly, and true,
but must it please me?
Luscious honey, purple rose, chocolate sky—
tell it all as if drunk.

13

Do not leave me, love.
Who can stare at your sun
and then sleep shine away?
You manipulate me, as sea beat/s ship,
to want, need, lust, have these chain/s.

Most would run;
one, sit still.

14

A man of woman/ly likeness said:
of diamond, of fluff;
like club, or like petal;
for use as to/y, & mean as an/y boy;
I am two, together.

15

So he ask/ed:
how does your trip go?

They trudge by butt/es,
swim fast/est, in place,
never stop to eat,
were size/d, shot at, hit, cook/'d,

but only in their head.

16

Here, we did
put a_s/top to them,
and

get rip/er produce by pound,
have some, take less, rob none,
want out!

Those see/r/s are gone.
No read/er has an/y recall.
Time is through.

Do y/ou_s/ing?

Random Words

From Kristine F: *euphoria, necropsy, sinecure*

The Gigolo's Lament

Do not be jealous of my sinecure.
The yield from this enforced euphoria
will leave no relics for a necropsy.

From Kristine F: *supernal, farthingale, cavil, abeyance*

The Vow

Do not cavil, sir, at my most grave resolve
to quarantine this heart in strict abeyance.
Neither smile, nor tear, nor saucy farthingale
shall vault the bar of my supernal calm.

From Kristine F: Sonnet, using *regatta, choleric, garrulous, dialectic, prattle, hirsute, placid, conundrums, jocose, qui-vive, junket, vouchsafe, weal, dolt*

Shall I Wax Choleric?

Shall I wax choleric, cursing the gold-spooned brats
who seize our common gifts as their private weal,
or, placid as a martyr, love the cats
vouchsafed to us by Caesar for our meal?

Shall I sport motley, saddened, yet jocose,
mocking the slimy junkets of our age,
or, like a sophist, professionally garrulous,
spin conundrums for a subsistent wage?

Qui-vive? What comic Jacobite might be left
pounding like a mulish dolt on an iron door?
Neither rage, nor prayer, nor prattle can arrest
the dialectic of the rich and poor.

Better luck, hirsute by art, to stay the grave
in endless regattas over complacent waves.

From Kristine F: *trouble, por qué, solstice, gulled, browbeaten, thug*

You Trouble My Dreams

You trouble my dreams, now, with the clearness of your eyes.
Por qué? I did not ask for the pleasure of this pain.
From solstice to solstice I have lain drugged with sorrow, until,
like a child easily gulled on April fool's day,
I have been tricked awake, browbeaten by desire,
while your beauty, like a thug, escapes my just embrace.

From Kristine F: *gam, mundane, lanai, wanton, megalopolis*

The Lanai

When the vast megalopolis extends the comfort of its
                              shrivelled arms,
pleading the passionate mundane, oh flee with me my love!
There, like innocent wantons west of the iron gate,
I will trace a lazy finger along your delicate gam,
languid, in a shaded lanai, the lost garden found.

From Annette K: *trophobiosis, quodlibet, propaedeutic, demarche, venire, apotropaic, eudaemonic, exorcise*

The New Symposium

From whence my desire? Shall we convene a new Symposium,
assemble a tipsy venire of sophists and stumbling playwrights,
to tussle with this quodlibet over strong wine?

Stuart drinks to the eudaemonic use of pleasure;
John's toasts are for apotropaic married love;
Charles hails the trophobiosis of kindly lust.

But no! This philosophical demarche is sure to fail!
Neither propadeutic blather, nor besotted wisdom
can ease the agenbite within, nor exorcise
these haunting intimations of a distant joy.

From Kristine F: *altercation, balk, curmudgeon, altruistic*

The Altruist

A *curmudgeon* you call me! Yes! I have never yet
balked at wasting my wit's precious ichor
in savage altercations with the world soul.
An altruist, I spill this wine for all.

From Kristine F: *fallacious, egregious, effigy, fastidious, garrulous*
From the dictionary, at random: *collar, embroider, heartily, remember, submersion*

The Heart's Rough Traces

The heart's rough traces cheat the fastidious mind.
How shall I collar this beast within? Shameless,
egregious in tears and laughter, it thrusts its rude
tongue, the garrulous gossip, into my formal
tea—Remember! Remember! Remember! Remember!

Better to wallow heartily, with a rich
submersion in the drippings rendered by fire
from our memory's fallacious flesh!—Until
this effigy, igniting in its own excess,
burns through to the unembroidered bones.

From Candice C: *raucous, disillusion, up, simmer*

My Disillusion

My disillusion, like a dubious egg,
simmered dully in the copper pot.
Turn up the heat! Now I must harden all
to a cold, white eye, in raucous boil.

From Kristin B: *orange, ocean, daisy, soap*

The Scent of You

As the rinds of a fat orange ravage my nails,
                after the sweet flesh is all consumed;
as ocean salt, embedded in our chafes,
                burns after the rough joy is over;
as the ichor from cut stems stains our jeans,
                while the necklaces of daisy lie discarded;
though our love is dead, the blackest pumice soap
                cannot scrape away the scent of you.

From Kristin B: *waterpolo, phone, sky, movie, running, choir, record, story*

Ordinary Joy

Saturday morning I played waterpolo; after the goal I gasped
                for breath; my eyes stung with chorine.
Then I phoned my buddy; we bragged, and joked, and bragged,
                while plotting the noon matinee.
My hair froze when I got outside; the light hurt;
                the new snow was brighter than the sky.
And at *Day of the Triffids* I was glad I could see it all—
                the meteors, the Borealis, the vast fields of
                              murderous plants.

After the show I was late for practice, as usual, running and slipping
                on the hidden mirrors, laughing and out of breath.
Choir was fun too, my voice was yet unbroken, and the girl
                in the second row of the second sopranos, she
                              smiled at me.
Later I listened to one of my dad's' records—*Hits of the Blitz*, I think.
                It was kind of funny, and kind of sad.

Then I slept. This is my story. This is your story.
                This is the chronicle of ordinary joy.

From Ann B: Sonnet, with acrostic, using *pipette, fidget, pork rind, Mother Theresa*

To Science Wed

Tell me, oh Muse, how might my words best vault
Or undermine these walls? That prize within,
Dearest to me, is deaf to my assault,
Resisting every overture to sin.

A Mother Theresa of Truth, to Science wed!
Neither mask of pork-rind chewing plain-spoke Yank,
Nor pose as sweet, sincere Canuck has led
Beyond her ramparts or astride her flank.

A golden world then, although naught but air,
Richer by far than truth, I shall create!
By subtle rhymes insinuating near,
I'll tempt her as she fidgets her pipette!

Even schoolgirls, who know their right from wrong,
Rush, always, to the truer lies of song.

Songs Without Ears

Heraclitus the Dark

Verse 1
They used to say
the world comes from water.
They used to say
the world comes from air.
But I say
it comes from a spark.
That's why they call me
Heraclitus the Dark.

Verse 2
Did I hear you say
you're going to the river?
Did I hear you say
you're going swimming at the bend?
Well let me say
it's not the same river.
You'll never see
the same river again.

Chorus 1
And the way up
is the way down.
And the way up
is the way down.
And the way up
is the way down.
And the way up
is the way down.

Verse 3
Why don't you listen?
Listen to the thunder.
Listen to it roll.
Listen to it peal.
Why aren't you looking?
Looking at the lightning?
Thunder and lightning:
always at the wheel.

Chorus 2
Where's the water?
It's flowing all around you.
Where's the air?
It's flowing all around you.
Where's the fire?
It's flowing all around you.
Where's the earth?
Changing, it rests.

Verse 4
Where's the music?
I can't feel the rhythm.
Where's the tune?
It's so hard to find.
It's not out in front.
It's not in the middle.
The harmony is stronger
when it comes from behind.

Chorus 1

Verse 5
You better wake up,
and take a look out at nature.
Better wake up,
and look at nature inside.
Better wake up;
you better look a little closer.
'Cause we love looking,
but nature loves to hide.

Chorus 2

Good

Verse 1
Nothing but a promise will convince me,
but I'm skeptical.
Nothing but a word could set it right.
Nothing but your voice will reassure me,
but I'm skeptical:
Why don't you promise to be good?

Chorus
Aren't you good?
You lied to me.
I thought you were good.
Aren't you good?
You lied to me.
I thought you were good.

Verse 2
Lying by my love all morning,
romantical.
Lying by my love all afternoon.
She loves me. So she tells me. But she's a liar,
hypocritical:
Too lazy to find something better to do.

Chorus
Was it good
to lay with me?
Wasn't it good?

Was it good
to lay with me?
Wasn't it good?

Verse 3
Nothing but a promise could redeem you,
but I'm skeptical.
Nothing but a word gives you away.
I knew it when I heard you chanting poetry,
heretical:
Evil, be thou my good.

Chorus
I'm so good!
Too good for you.
I'm so good!
I'm so good!
Too good for you.
I'm so good!

It's a Mystery

Verse 1
She makes me wonder
how I could ever be the same.
My life before her is a mystery.
I can't remember
what it was like to be alone.
I think I'll keep it a mystery.

Verse 2
She brings the child;
she brings the man out in me.
She brings out both, simultaneously.
She makes me stronger;
she makes me weak in the knees.
How does she do it? It's a mystery.

Chorus
It's a mystery, a mystery,
a mystery to me,
(etc.)

Verse 3
I think I know her,
no more surprises left for me,
and then I'm baffled by a mystery.
I get so angry,
and she gets angrier at me.
Why did she leave? It's a mystery.

Chorus

Bridge
I don't want to, but I want to,
and I don't want to discover.
I don't want to, but I want to,
and I don't want to uncover.
I don't' want to, but I want to,
and I don't want to recover.
I don't want to, but I want to,
and I don't want to love her.

Verse 4
Some say tomorrow
is impossible to see.
Some say the future is a mystery.
I went to Delphi,
and I asked what is to be.
She said *Love is a mystery.*

Chorus

Talking to Tomorrow

Verse 1
The early light calls to me: *Awaken.*
Can't you see the sun resurrecting?
She holds me tight. I shake her off.
Got a dream to fight, and no time to talk.
She never believes my prophecies.

Verse 2
At work the thought occurs I'm mistaken.
Is there something I've forgotten or forsaken?
A thirty year retirement plan,
social security—
Yes, I can retire in paradise.

Chorus
All my life I've tried to
keep a wary eye, or two,
to the future.
But every time a vision calls
I linger, and the future falls
into the past.
I don't have time to talk to you.
I'm talking to tomorrow,
talking to tomorrow,
talking to tomorrow,
talking to tomorrow.

Verse 3
After class a student calls: *Oh teacher,*
I want to learn your every thought, your every feature.
Come; listen; take my impression;
promise me to give it to a future generation.
I'll be living in you, tomorrow.

Chorus

Verse 4
At night I fear my sleep; I fear my waking,
the present, past, and future, ever changing.
I crawl to the cabinet and swallow my fears.
Make me a prophet. Make me a seer.
Tonight will be tomorrow, forever.

Chorus

The Boston Company Anthem

Verse 1
We will never love you.
We will never hate you.
That is why we have your trust.
But we will always like you.
We will be your friend.
After all, we hold your cash.

Chorus
'Cause we are not *a* company.
'Cause we are not a *Boston* Company.
'Cause we are *The*, are *The*, are *The*
Boston Company.

Verse 2
Back in the 80s
things were very good,
in the indulgent arms of American Express.
Now it's the 90s;
things are better still.
We have merged with a piece of fruit.

Chorus

Verse 3
Our crafty sales staff
have many devices
to help you favor funds you never knew you'd ever savor.

Our money managers
are our planetary guides,
governed by intelligences real and artificial.

Chorus

Verse 4
We've got buildings,
like OBP,
CSC, CSC, et La Place D'Exchange.
We've got acronyms,
like TBC;
best of all is AMGIIIAMI.

Chorus

Verse 5
Yes, we have suffered
the acrid pain
of a child betrayed by his dear papa.
But like a serpent,
we have shed our skin.
Naked, new, this snake shall strike!

Chorus

The Investment Manager's Promise

Strophe
When the trumps of gold resound,
our vigilance will be there.
When the graying sage expounds,
our vision endows his chair.
When the poor and sick lie crying,
our councils relieve despair,
tomorrow's shocks confounding
with the providence of our care.

Antistrophe
The world can be a carnival of chance,
our wretched lives the fee;
and at the wheel, the Dismal Science
spins with antic glee.
And through this maze of vanity and fear
the errant mind beseeches
longingly
for a guide.

Strophe
When the worthy stock lies wounded,
our patronage will uphold.
When the battered firm arouses
our confidence will embold.
When the fettered coin lies dungeoned,
we will melt that cross of gold,
and the hopes of a thousand dreamers
our munificence enfold.

Johnny and Sue

Gather round me, every one.
Hear a story 'bout a foolish man.
And when the story comes to an end,
try to forget it, if you can.
Oh, oh, if you can.

Johnny wanted to fuck with Sue.
But Johnny wanted his freedom too.
Sue got pregnant. Johnny flew.
Well he had to. Wouldn't you?
Oh, oh, wouldn't you?

Johnny wanted to get a job.
He remembered his friend Bob.
So he called him, and he got
a great position. Thanks a lot.
Oh, oh, thanks a lot.

Johnny wanted to write a song,
not too short, and not too long.
Threw out everything that didn't belong.
Made a million. Is that so wrong?
Oh, oh, is that so wrong?

Johnny wanted to die well,
without pain, or a smell,
with a fortune when he fell.
Now he's the richest man in hell.
Oh, oh, in hell.

The Derivatives of Love

Verse 1
I sit across the desk from you,
hoping for a second look.
I drink my coffee close to you,
reading an impressive book.
But you never say another word to me
but a blank, polite, hello.
Why are you so busy with buying and selling?
Can't you feel my heart, dying slow?

Chorus
Let's play the derivatives of love.
Let's bet on the future of our merger.
Stock that is low will rise above,
and you shall profit from my resurgence.

Verse 2
In the ivy bowers, back at school,
all the girls whispered my name.
And now in Boston's finest bars,
all the women whisper the same,
'cause I'm a handsome, Harvard-educated man,
and sure to be a great success.
But I'd trade every one of my amorous hours
for a moment of your tenderness.

Chorus

Verse 3
I saw you talking on the phone
and I couldn't help but overhear;
your boho boyfriend's back in town,
after neglecting you for a year.
Well don't be fooled by his artsy-fartsy ways;
he's nothing but an ignorant beast.
And don't be distracted by my mastery of money;
in my tender heart I'm a true artiste.

Chorus

Verse 4
Someday we'll look back on this
with a happy, ironic smile,
amazed that our conjugal bliss
was founded on financial wile.
So please buy an option on my worth;
maturity will see it rise.
I'll bet a fortune on the future of your love,
and we'll watch our profits realize.

Chorus

Texas Wind

Chorus
I'm sitting in the warm Texas wind,
waiting for the storm that's coming in.
It's going to rain hard, but it won't rain long,
and when the thunder passes through,
I'll be gone.

Verse 1
I was born in Decatur, the heart of the state,
by the scissortail's path and the possum's lake,
the youngest son of a poor estate,
itching to wrestle with the arms of fate.
So I joined the navy and fled my home;
like a restless pioneer, I roamed.
But a life of wandering, all alone,
was a little too cold for me.

Chorus

Verse 2
Then I met a woman, from far Japan,
who was more than a match for this rambling man.
I fell in love, tried to settle down,
with wife and family in corporate land.
So I climbed the lines and I climbed the rungs
of the corporate ladder and the corporate dung,
'til the fancy smiles and rattlesnake's tongues
were a little too much for me.

Chorus

Verse 3
So I quit my job and I found a place
in the land of the star and the open space,
and I spend my hours in a headlong race,
testing the limits of heavenly grace.
I lost my money, and I lost my wife,
but I've got my hook and my Bowie knife,
and I found the spring that waters my life
flowing beneath my feet.

Chorus

Verse 4
They say I've the cancer, and already half dead
from too little sleep and too many cigarettes,
but the sting isn't bad and my only regret
is the smirk on the face of the card-shark Death.
But while we were playing I gave him a run,
made him fight like the devil for every point he won,
and no other soul was nearly as fun
to wrestle underground as me.

Chorus

Verse 5
Don't worry my daughters; your dad'll be fine.

I'm going where the crappies are always on the line,
a deer's in the freezer, a turkey in my sights
and always a card game playing through the night,
where a man can have family, and girlfriends too,
a 9 to 5 job, and yet nothing to do,
where nothing is wanting, well nothing but you,
nothing but you.

Chorus

Trip West

I left behind
the old job.
I left behind
the old home.

I crossed the desert.
I climbed the mountain.
I stumbled
to the sea.

In spite of
the census
of the year
1890,

in spite of
the scholar,
Mister Frederick
Jackson Turner,

the American
frontier
will never
close.

We are all
on a perpetual
trip
west.

Kristine

Verse 1
I was all alone.
I was far from home,
wondering if she would come home to me,
or sink me, like a stone.
Then I saw your face,
like a flower floating on the sea,
like first love's sweet memory,
like a whispered grace.

Chorus
Kristine: why'd you work your way under my skin?
Kristine: can't you see the mess I'm in?
Kristine: it really isn't much of a sin, Kristine.
Kristine: why'd you work your way under my skin?
Kristine: can't you see the mess I'm in?
Kristine: it's only a venial sin, Kristine.

Verse 2
I was safe and low,
in San Diego, under six feet of snow,
way down deep, where nobody could go;
guess I didn't know.
It isn't hard to see
how a broken lover like me
could find in your eyes, a haven, where he
could lie, without pain.

Chorus
Kristine: why'd you work your way under my skin?
Kristine: can't you see the mess I'm in?
Kristine: it really isn't much of a sin, Kristine.
Kristine: why'd you work your way under my skin?
Kristine: can't you see the mess I'm in?
Kristine: let's pay the wages of sin, Kristine.

Verse 3
I know you can't be mine;
it isn't the place; it'll never be the time.
May and September can never align;
I know that's true.
Forgive me, if you can,
the foolish dreams of a middle-aged man.
I lost it all once, and I'll lose it again,
before I'm through.

Chorus
Kristine: why'd you work your way under my skin?
Kristine: can't you see the mess I'm in?
Kristine: it really isn't much of a sin, Kristine.
Kristine: why'd you work your way under my skin?
Kristine: can't you see the mess I'm in?
Kristine: let's try an original sin, Kristine.

Greenhead

Verse 1
Under the sun, by the sea,
on the strand of history,
with a *G* and an *A* and a *T* and a *C*,
nature played a trick on me.

Chorus
Greenhead.
Greenhead.
Greenhead.
Greenhead.

Verse 2
I was born in a pizza pie.
Maggots were my family.
I can fuck, but I can't cry.
When the moon wanes, I will die.

Chorus

Verse 3
I've got six; you've got four.
You've got two; I've got more.
I can breathe through my pores.
I can fly and you can crawl.

Bridge
Help me.
Help me.
Help me.
Help me.

Verse 4
I may be an arthropod,
living on borrowed blood,
but I'm free of the rod,
and nagging of your whining god.

Chorus

Pannikin

Verse 1
There's a little grey shack, near the sea,
with a bench or two that's always free,
where I like to spend a lazy afternoon,
drinking coffee, sipping tea,
sitting quietly, but never lonely,
never lonely.

Chorus
I'm panickin'; I'm panickin',
'cause I'm in love with the girls
at Pannikin; I'm panickin',
'cause I'm in love.

Verse 2
They've been there since 1974,
the boho girls I'm looking for,
with smiles, and flowers in their hair.
There's Shawna, and Lucille,
and Eleanor, and Adrian.
Did you hear that Adrian?

Chorus

Bridge
My heart is aching.
My will is breaking.

My legs are shaking.
Save me.

Verse 3
I know my hair's a little bit grey
and I've got a crick in my back;
and I might crush you
when I have my heart attack;
but Picasso, had Marie,
and Ulysses, had Calypso.
Be my Calypso.

Chorus

Burn On

(with Marco Martinez)

Verse 1
In the house I was born
there's a plain little room,
with a lock on the door,
where I used to go
when I couldn't bear
to hear any more.

Chorus
You've got to go on.
You've got to burn on.
You've got to go on, and on, and on.

Verse 2
Then one happy day
it all went away.
My mom was in pain,
'cause daddy was gone.
We were left on our own.
Better off on our own.

Chorus

Verse 3
You've heard it before:
this plain little tale
of love going wrong,
and a child in fear.
But one thing is new:
the child is you.

Chorus

Turnaround
(with Marco Martinez)

Verse 1
I'm sitting here alone, thinking of the words
to write you, so far away.
And in each word, I can see your eyes,
softer than the night.
And maybe you'll cry, when you think of me,
and wonder why you left.
And maybe you'll smile, above the pain,
and think it was for the best.

Chorus
But I got my feet back on the ground.
And I've waited so long
for this turnaround.
And I've waited so long
for this turnaround.

Verse 2
I used to believe that the pain I've seen
could never happen to us.
And I thought that rings and promises
could keep you in my arms.
But now I've learned, when it comes to love,
love is not enough.

Chorus

Verse 3
I know I never understood
your restlessness.
And I hope you're right that living apart
is for the best.
And I hope that pain is a lot like love,
and comes to an end.

Chorus

Cold

Verse 1
I saw the first green leaves of spring.
It left me cold.
I heard the love-sick robin sing.
It left me cold.
I felt the raindrops gathering;
I heard the dark clouds thundering;
I saw the storm lash everything,
wash away the winter's sin.
It left me . . .

Chorus
Cold.
Cold.
Cold.
Cold.

Verse 2
I saw a child sing on the street.
It left me cold.
I paid a busker for a melody.
It left me cold.
I heard a choral fantasy,
a swollen Mahler symphony;
I felt the serpent's agonies;
I heard an angel call to me.
It left me . . .

Chorus

Verse 3
A bashful virgin smiled at me.
It left me cold.
A jaded whore blushed for me.
It left me cold.
A beautiful woman fell for me.
She spread her legs, to satisfy me.
She opened her arms to comfort me,
proclaiming endless love.
She left me.

She's So Sad

Verse 1
She's so sad.
She's so finicky.
She thinks the world should kneel
before her divinity.
She's so cold.
She's so serious.
Why must every word
be so damn mysterious?

Chorus
I don't care.
I don't care.
I don't care.
I don't care.

Verse 2
She's got lips,
hot like licorice.
She's got a devils kiss,
that feels like innocence.
She's got hips,
tight as an anchoress,
and slim angelic arms.
She's insidious.

Chorus

Verse 3
Been here before.
Did I learn my lesson?
You'd think I'd need
no second guessing.
But she talks like a poet,
and she walks like a whore,
and maybe if I treat her bad
it'll even the score.

Chorus

Not Afraid

Verse 1
I want a girl who's not afraid
to climb in the back of my white Corolla,
of dogs in the street, of ants in my pantry,
of the weight of words on thin white paper.
I want a girl who's not afraid
of the big bad boss and his thin white lines,
of the dizzying depth of the pit sublime,
of the sadness that burns in the white of my eyes.

Chorus
Not afraid,
not afraid,
not afraid,
I'm not afraid.

Verse 2
I want a brother who's not afraid
of the bully who's trying to steal my candy,
of the fish that's bleeding on the hook,
of the voices that call me under the bed.
I want a brother who's not afraid
of the wild boars in the big black forest,
of spitting out the wafer and wine,
of taking apple's from daddy's tree.

Chorus

Verse 3
I want to be not afraid
of a slap from dad, of a frown from mummy,
of getting caught with my hands on the money,
of making her mad, of making her happy.
I want to be not afraid
of cheap paint on a blank canvas,
of looking up a word in a rhyming dictionary,
of saying what I think when I'm really not thinking.

Chorus

I Didn't do Nothing

Verse 1
I was minding my own business,
sitting at the bar,
one hand on a whiskey,
and one on my guitar,
when I saw her sitting
way too close to me.
She asked me for a drink.
She didn't ask about the ring.
She asked me back to her place
just to hear me sing.
So I said ok.
I said ok.
She'll never know,
anyway.

Verse 2
I was walking down the street
with a lot on my mind;
I was running out of money;
I was running out of time,
when I saw him lying
in that alley way.
Maybe he was sick.
Maybe he was drunk.
He could've been my brother.

He could've been a bum.
But I ain't no doctor,
and I ain't no cop.
So I walked on by.
I walked on by.

Verse 3
I was hanging with the boys,
having us some fun,
shooting off our mouths,
shooting off our guns.
It was crazy Billy
had the mad idea.
We only meant to scare 'im,
and put 'im in his place,
far from his betters
with that smile off his face.
I didn't mean to see 'im
hanging from that tree.
But I didn't do nothing.
No, not me.

Keith Wanted

Verse 1
Keith wanted
to look like a player.
He wanted to look
like a dangerous fellar.
But he was sweet
as the port in my cellar.
Keith wanted
to be Norman Mailer.

Chorus
But what Keith really wants
is only to love
the woman that he's
thinking of.

Verse 2
Keith danced
at the club Anaconda,
giving the eye
to the girl in the corner.
She gave him a treat
in the back of her Honda.
One more girl,
but not the one that he wanna.

Chorus

Verse 3
Now Keith's
run off to Sonoma,
looking for smiles,
and looking for soma,
but neither the sun,
nor the winy aroma,
can wake Keith up
from his romantic coma.

Chorus

Sixty Years

Verse 1
She was waiting for a train in Brantford station.
I was waiting to fly in the war.
If I didn't chase her, to steal that kiss
I might never get a chance anymore.
I took her up for a ride in the Piper.
The wind made a mess of her hair.
It was a wonderful way to say goodbye;
then the bastards cancelled the war!

Chorus
Sixty years, in the kitchen,
sixty years, in the ring,
sixty years, in the garden,
sixty years, sixty years.

Verse 2
We were stationed in twenty different cities,
from Langar to Goose Bay.
We lived in twenty different PMQ's,
and every damn one looked the same.
She hung out her washing on the Siegfried Line.
She ironed by the Labrador moon.
We whispered an oath to the RCAF
and slept through another sonic boom.

Chorus

Verse 3
I don't know how we paid for the groceries.
I don't know how we paid for the togs.
And I hope all those years of college
taught 'em kids cost a lot more than dogs.
And two became teachers of children,
and one stayed in Ottawa, eh?
And one plays all night with his old guitar,
and one plays with chips by the Bay.

Chorus

Verse 4
Now time's a jealous little bugger.
He can't stand the happiness he sees.
He fiddled with my heart, then stole my hips,
and now he's threatening her knees.
But we don't care what happens tomorrow.
We don't bother with fear or regret.
'Cause nothing can take what's in our heart,
and nothing can make us forget.

Chorus

I Wished Her Dead

Verse 1
It started like it started
a million times before.
She said a little something.
I said a little more.
I knew how to be cold.
I knew how to be cruel.
She knew how to hurt me,
and make me feel a fool.

Verse 2
I should have laughed it off,
like every other time.
She'd be in my arms.
I'd be on her mind.
But something changed,
and I don't know what,
but deep inside
a door slammed shut.

Chorus
I wished her dead,
and the last leaf fell from the tree.
I wished her dead,
and then it all happened to me.
I wished her dead,
and I found what it meant to be free.
I wished her dead.

Verse 3
Now I'm finally free,
free to do as I dare,
free to have who I want,
and free not to care.
But no matter who
I lie beside,
no matter how warm,
I feel cold inside.

Verse 4
'Cause you can ask for fame,
you can ask for gold,
pray you get the girl,
pray you don't get old.
But be careful what you wish for
'cause it might come true—
not the way you thought it,
but the way it thought you.

Chorus

The Immolation

When I See the Lark
(Bernard de Ventadorn, c. 1145-1180)

When I see the lark, with joy,
thrust its wings into the sun,
falling, as his will allows,
in sweet oblivion,
with envy I am wrought
for all I see in happiness,
and marvel that desire does not
melt my heart like wax.

Alas, I thought I knew
this Love, but do not know enough
to hold myself from loving her,
though she will give me nought.
She has, besides herself,
my heart, my soul, and all the world,
for me—nothing—after she left,
but longing in the blood.

I lost all power of choice
the hour I became her toy,
when she let me gaze into her eyes,
the mirrors of my joy.
Oh Mirror, since I saw
myself in you, I have been slain
by sighs, and now am lost, like fair
Narcissus at the stream.

I have no hope in women,
and I will put no trust in them;
indeed, I will in turn abandon
those I did once defend.
For I can see none here
who counters her destruction;
I doubt them all, and all I fear,
for they are all as one.

Well she's a woman, and that
is what I fault my lady for,
because she wants what she should not,
and does what I abhor.
I follow an ill star,
playing the fool on the bridge,
and aimless as a wanderer
through clouds above the ridge.

To look at her one might
not once imagine that she'd let
this wretch, withering out of sight,
die without her help.
Mercy is lost, it is sure.
Indeed, I always was bereft
of all I should have won from her,
and there's no mercy left.

And since nor prayer nor pity
helps me seize my rights from her,
and since this love can't make her happy
I shall no longer tell her,

but leave her, and renounce her,
free from service and revile!
She has slain me; death is my answer,
a wanderer in exile.

Tristan! No more songs
from me; I'm off! Where I'll be staying,
who knows? Somewhere free from pain,
or joy, or love, in hiding.

I Wish My Arms

I wish my arms were long enough
to hold you now,
my absent love.

I wish my dreams were big enough
to enfold you
in a cloudy sleep.

I wish my heart was deep enough
to drown you
in my love.

I wish the world was wide enough
to walk with you
the bounds of my desire.

The Sky Asked

The sky asked:
Where is my sacrifice?
The earth expelled
another age of bones.

The monarch asked:
Where is my tribute?
The people sent to him
a crowned head on a gilded mirror.

The lover asked:
Where is your mercy, and my tears?
She opened her eyes.
She did not look at him.

Aubade

The sun is rising now, over
our little blue shack, and now reveals
the innocent translucence of your skin,
and all the pretty freckles you tried to hide.

There is another world of beauty underneath
your perfect form, beneath the still more perfect
power of your art. I feel it now
in the beating of your open heart.

I have told so many lies, to you
and to myself, and all because
I did not want to hurt you. No—
I did not want to lose you, showing

in too harsh a light, that underneath
this shoulder where you rest your cheek
as I whisper poetry in your delicate ear
is a wounded beast, rutting in the dark.

Why can't the sun stay put, just
for a little while longer, while its soft
morning light, and your soft cheek, smooth
the ragged, secret chambers of my heart?

But the day won't stop for me, or anyone.
Noon comes, dark falls, and every truth will out.
I am left, at last, with a familiar plea:
I love you. Forgive me. Come back to me.

Anabelly Blues

The birds sing every morning. Why can't I?
The birds sing every morning. Why can't I?
There's dew on the grass. But I'm still dry.

I used to complain, 'cause my bed was too small.
I used to complain, 'cause my bed was too small.
Now there's too much space between me and the wall.

I don't know why, but I miss her voice.
I don't know why, but I miss her voice.
She was too much trouble. Now there's too much peace.

There's a worm crawling, naked on the walk.
There's a worm crawling, naked on the walk.
That same worm's crawling through my naked heart.

Cedar Fire

You might think we were on mars, choking
on a red fog, while black spots stain the sun.
But it's just another day on this familiar earth,
just another natural disaster, more kindling
for the morning news, 'til firemen, and weathermen
snuff it out. That brightness gone, we sate ourselves
on the survivors sifting hopelessly through ashen
leaves, dead deer, lost wives, and cracked foundations.

I don't know anyone who was right there, but I do
know somebody who knew somebody, and for them
it hurt, and will never stop burning, though time and need
will thicken the scars inside, until they stagger on,
looking, pretty much, exactly like the rest of us.

Tears extinguish nothing, not even our own
grief, though it is natural to mourn for those
close to our heart, and merciful, perhaps,
that after dreams, children, pets, and property
the flood exhausts itself. Only a god

has pity enough to weep the immolation
of sons and sparrows both. The rest of us
must do our duty still, as if we did not feel
at all, fearing our restless heart while yet
we honor it. We die by nature, or by duty,
but we must live for both.

Winter Solstice

The sun comes back once more, as is its old
habit, and once again you have returned
to my unworthy arms. Yes, you have told
me a thousand times, and so far I have learned

nothing, for still my stubborn heart looks back
to the comfortable wounds that yet remain,
like a pagan to his withering god, racked
in an everlasting sacrament of pain.

Drape your black hair before these faithless eyes,
my love, and let that night eclipse the past.
Enlist the mathematics of your thighs
in a bold proof, that will make manifest,

even to my dogmatic witlessness,
the axiomatic clarity of your embrace.

The Little White Dog

And the little white dog
remains
the little white dog,
beside
the black trash can,
depending
entirely on me.

And the big peach rose
smells
like the big peach rose.

And the golden snake
bites his own tail
again.

And everything reminds me
of things that remind themselves
of nothing.

The dog won't fetch.
Nothing will move this mind to rest.

Redondillas
(Sor Juana Inés de la Cruz, 1651–1695)

Idiot men, who would disdain
all women, and without a thought
to how you are, yourselves, at fault
precisely for the sins you blame!

Your irrepressible desire
feels no shame at our contempt,
yet mocks, when our concupiscence
melts, at last, before your fire.

You pummel all resistance, then
assert, with false solemnity,
that lightness, and frivolity,
with scarce a fight, just let you in!

The boldness of your mad conceit
reminds me of the boy who made
a bogey out of sticks and hay,
then gave himself an awful fright.

In your presumption, like an ass,
you hope for women who could be
like bashful Thaís while they flee,
but hot Lucrecia in your grasp.

Could a man be any more bereft
of every trace of common sense,

taking ridiculous offence
at a mirror fogged with his own breath?

You weigh our favor and disdain
equally, in your cockeyed scale,
for if we love you, how you rail!
And if we scorn, how you complain!

The most prudent woman's nothing but,
(according to your harsh decrees)
the while she keeps you out, a tease
and when she lets you in, a slut.

Your lunatic democracy
levels the castle and the ditch;
one woman's called a cruel bitch,
another one an easy lay.

And after your seductive taunts
coax soft limbs to liberty,
you wish we fallen angels be
tightly bound as living saints.

Indeed, though you take pleasure in
touting your anger and your pain,
lucky is she who can refrain
from love, while you complain, complain!

How might a woman, then, be mixed,
to be worthy of your grudging love,
if the ungrateful, you reprove,
and the easy ones just leave you vexed?

And who has earned the stiffest rap
for love's unlicensed liberties:
the woman collapsing at his pleas,
or the rascal pleading from her lap?

Or who, the keenest bite within,
(though either would be wise to pray)
the woman sinning for her pay
or the man paying for his sin?

And why are you dismayed at the
immoral debts of your estate?
Love the women you create,
Or craft them as you'd have them be.

Give up, for once, this shameless egging
on, and then it might be just
to reprehend the foolish lust
of she who comes for seconds, begging.

With several arms, and subtle evil,
arrogance incites the battle,
your persistence, and your prattle,
wedding world, flesh, and devil.

Legitimate Form

Some poets believe
that the only legitimate form
for verse born to this disillusioned age
splits
the flowing limbs
along natural breaks.

And when each contraction
aches from within,
we must mark this partial birth
with a gap
yawning like the evacuating womb.

This reminds me very much, however,
of grade school,
parsing
the sentence into the stanza,
the phrase, the line.

Yes, this is *natural*,
like an infant's first words,
sauntering
in the primeval gait
our seed has decided for us.

But, all in all,
I prefer
an infant's cry.

Madrigal
(Gutierre de Cetina, 17th Century)

O clear, calm eyes,
if, for a sweet look, you merit praise,
why must you wither me with angry gaze?
If kindness will impress
your beauty in the glass of my desire,
do not glare, with painful ire,
lest such contempt sully your loveliness.
Oh torment ravenous!
O clear, calm eyes!
Won't you deign to look, at least, though you despise?

Hearts of Air
(with Gabriela Anaya Valdepeña)

Not gravity, nor fleshly gravitas,
nor doubt, nor shame, nor bashfulness, nor blight
burdens the amorous angels, while they pass
silently, limb through limb, as light through light.

Arms of cloud cannot tangle. Hearts of air
cannot break like the mournful tide against the reef.
Cold kisses cannot bind, nor can despair
clog super-lunar ears with songs of grief.

But here beneath the moon, my tousled hair,
scented with jasmine, drives your temples mad!
And my lips must promise all they can before
they press only the cold mortician's slab.

Yet if blood is mortal, and mortal is your kiss,
I will not trade this death for an angel's bliss.

Marriage, Like War

Marriage, like war, has many casualties.
And, as in war, the greatest sacrifice
falls to the young, whose maudlin fantasies
spur them onward to pay an awful price.

And when our wrinkled veterans press their luck,
returning to the field in spite of sense,
justly, with Doctor Johnson, do we mock
"the triumph of hope over experience."

And yet, while prudent eunuchs save their skin,
love-ridden fools seed this earth with blood.
Indeed, all future glories breed within
those heedless heroes wrestling in the mud.

Though weddings seem, to reason, simple terror,
nature has reason, yet, to praise our error.

The Conqueror

You cost me the gold hoarded from five sacked towns,
and the blood of fifty true retainers, spilled
in the taking of that gold. Still, I was sure
the price was worth it. I had never seen—
though I have known a thousand whores, maidens,
and concubines, all who yielded their pleasure
willingly to me, at the trifling price
of knowing only that I was their conqueror—
no, I had never seen a look like that!

And now I own you. You are waiting there
in my tent, your ivory skin caressed by silks
snatched from the palaces of Samarkand,
and scented with oils pressed from I know not what.
Yes, I own you; but I am not the I
who scoffed at love that took longer than a piss,
and would rather mount a bony battle steed
than linger at his mistress' perfumed toes.
Those pretty toes! That shroud of night-black hair!
You have unmanned me with the very force
that makes me man, and I no longer own
myself. They say that once a prince of Rome
gave up the pomp and plunder of half the world
for the narrow span of one Egyptian bed.
That tent shall be my prison, and there I shall
await the shame of another Actium.

We Can't Help It.

Why do we waste our time loving a dog,
a dumb animal, a drooling puking mess,
who whines after you, sappy eyes agog,
whenever you leave the house to dump the trash?

He kills no rats. He herds no sheep. He bites,
so far, no burglars in their burgling ass.
He does, however, sleep all day and night,
and chew his way right through my ready cash.

But we can't help it; his fathers, way back when,
gave up their freedom for a hunk of fat,
and he's trailed after us since, like a needy friend
who never leaves, and now we're used to it.

So maybe this affection's something that
we might as well accept, since it's a fact.

To My Father

Fifty-five years of fatherhood
cannot, I know, be understood
from the inside, by one like me,
a father, only belatedly,
who skipped first cries, first words, first walks,
measles, mumps, and the chicken pox,
and only now pays off arrears
by crashing into the teenage years,
while you have been, five times before,
a veteran of the entire war,
emerging from each battle-ground
victorious, with no visible wounds,
and having made, remarkably,
grateful friend of your enemy.

Perhaps you fear no medal's won
by feats familiar to everyone,
and wish you'd done some more of *this*,
and as for *that*, a little less,
but, without meaning to be contrary,
your doubts are quite imaginary—
Statistics show that, out of five,
one of us should be in the grave,
in prison, or in poverty,
or one of us, at least, should be
destroyed by hate, or jealousy,
and yet we've all defied the fates
with life, liberty, jobs, and mates,
and when we search our memories

find very few atrocities,
besides those times our growing tastes
were stunted by your *gluck on toast*,
or that one time, in 67,
at the great Canadian Exhibition,
when Brian pushed me, and I pushed back,
and you yelled at me, despite the fact
that simple justice forced my hand,
though now I think I understand—

Justice is never simple. You
have always tried to guide us through
a world where much remains obscure,
and much is hard, and nothing sure,
except that a little love can be
stronger than anything else. And we
can only hope to prove again
the truth that you've already shown.

The Passions of Jacques Batârd

(Contributions, as Jacques Batârd, to *Roses of Crimson Fire: an Epistolary Novel in Prose, Verse, and Image*, by Gabriela Anaya Valdepeña and Richard Denner.)

Alma, Jacques Batârd's beautiful and dangerously imaginative lover, insists upon participating in the Mills College Poetry Conference. Jacques cannot go, but is loath to deny her this pleasure. At the same time he is well aware, after a long history of adventure and misadventure in the company of versifying rascals, of the risks to which his dear Alma may be exposing herself, particularly if his old acquaintance Bouvard Pécuchet makes an appearance. The only available stratagem, he decides, is to enlist the aid of yet another rascal, Rychard Artaud, using a combination of measured pleas and subtle threats.

(Jacques Batârd to Rychard Artaud, May 24th, 2006)

I do not trust you, and I never have,
though circumstances must, at times, forgive
where friends would not. And we were friends, of sorts,
if borrowed bail discharged to sundry courts
could purchase friendship. Yes, all that was *then*,
but now I must, reluctantly, again
bet on your better nature. There is a woman
at stake. You smile, I'm sure, to see my human
weakness crest at such a trivial cause;
but Alma is nothing like the giddy sows
we'd fuck with in the bars of Malibu.
No, she is beauty, fire, and sweetness, too,
compact with wit and deep imagination—

but enough of that; I'll come to the summation:
she wishes to attend that conference
for poetry at Mills College where once
Bouvard and I contested to undo
the greatest share of eager ingenue
with glib iambics, metered masquerades,
bohemian masks, and lyrical charades.
And though my mighty Alma is more apt
to slay, herself, legions of fools rapt
in her own words, before she also die,
her fruitfulness of fancy might supply,
to subtle hands, a highway to her heart.
What can I do then? Any time apart,
however brief, corrodes me like a fire,
but neither can I come, nor can deny her.
So that leaves you, as the unlikely guard
'gainst all usurpers, not the least Bouvard,
who may well be there too. And, if you please,
do not let slip, to Alma, that a disease
of fellowship once infected he and I;
that is, although a fact I can't deny,
a diagnosis she need never know.
I hold you, then, responsible, Artaud,
for keeping Alma safe from all design,
and do not forget that, though, like the divine,
I cannot, or will not, orchestrate it all,
and Alma must, like Eve, be free to fall,
I have reserved, as jealous Yahweh hath,
innumerable objects for my wrath.

Jacques' threats and pleas notwithstanding, Rychard's friend Bouvard does indeed exercise his practiced charm, under the Mills Col-

lege moon, for the benefit of Jacques' lover Alma. But what happens when the charmer himself is charmed by his victim? Confused and fearful, Bouvard leaves the affair unconsummated, preferring the romance of unrequited epistolary expostulations to the dangerous intensities of an incarnate affair.

Jacques, however, while skeptical of love, has never flinched from the rush of blood, and finds their secret correspondence, upon its inevitable discovery, quite ridiculous. He responds with a short note of imperious contempt, slipping in a faded photograph to remind Bouvard of the true source of power, all the while hoping that Alma's affections will return, unreservedly, to himself:

(Jacques Batârd to Bouvard Pécuchet, September 28th, 2006)

She confessed to me, at last—this ridiculous
correspondence. I think she thought I cared, but she
could no more leave me than her heart could leave
her ribs, we are that tangled, she and I.
I was a poet once, like you Bouvard,
before I understood that the cold force
of my imperious will alone could bend
bones and steel as efficiently as words.
And that was when I left you fools behind,
with your paper castles, to ink my own epic
in cum, powder, blood, and the Congo River.
And now, after all I've seen, and after all
I've done, this little skit is nothing more
than children playing on Sunday afternoon.
Children, poets, eunuchs, you're all the same!
And when my little Alma is all through,
and crying with exhaustion, I will take her

into my time-scarred arms, scolding, mocking,
and comforting at once, until she sleeps
or weeps herself into oblivion.

Bouvard shares this note with Rychard, who responds on Bouvard's behalf with a mixture of mollification and friendly amusement. At the same time, he warns Jacques to "circumambulate this mandala

with care." Even if Bouvard, "at this stage in his rebirth," is not yet
his match, he is nevertheless the product of "Tibetan and Talmudic
magic."

"Love is stronger than fear," Rychard adds, suggesting that Alma
may have been driven to "these excesses" by Jacques himself. And
Jacques must surely know that Alma is "a high priestess," whose
voice "sings beyond the beauty of the sea, a cry not ours." Jacques,
however, knows no sorcery but the power of reason, in the service of
a transforming will, and responds in the measured rumble of dac-
tylic hexameter:

(Jacques Batârd to Rychard Artaud, September 29th, 2006)

I have received your letter, Artaud, though why I bother
answering you, or Jampa, or even that shrunken fool
Bouvard, who fancies himself my rival, this might clarify—
Even a bull, with blood-heavy sceptres of iron, and crown
of horn, still bothers to tail-whip pestering clouds of gnats!
And I'm glad you love the décor, and the feathery cap. I keep
forgetting how all these trappings may seem exotic, or comic,
perhaps, to those who know but glimpses of foreign manners
in moldering movies, or drug-addled visions of Marrakech.
But me, I have lived them, until I grew weary with them all,
like a housewife stuck in the suburbs. And nowhere was
                                                                      there sorcery;
nothing but ignorance—that and the man who knows a few
                                                                            tricks,
although I may just know a few more, Artaud, than you!
And as for that golem, Pécuchet, I may credit his power
much more than you might wager, for I have seen ironwood
                                                                           fetishes
polished and potent as he, and they seemed to glower with all

the reflected force that a thousand credulous eyes could
lend them.
Still, they burned like trash when I tossed them into the fire.
Nor am I the vicious nabob that murderous rumor trumpets
(though sometimes it serves me well when fools will reckon
me thus!).
You have noticed the softness around these eyes, which
might be thought
to sparkle indulgently, while with child-like spells you ache
to fashion the slattern night in the shape of your velvet desires.
But do you imagine that they would willingly watch her
leave me?
I love her, and love to indulge her, yes, and yes, I have learned,
through the bitterest wastes of passion, one cannot compel
desire.
But do not forget what I have learned, as well—if we master
our own dark lusts, we will never again be scared of the dark.
You may call it my pride, my indifference, the strength of
my own deep sadness,
but this black strength within me blooms with the power to
choke,
along with my bruised affections, the cries of pity herself.
You tell me that love is stronger than fear? That is not my
experience.
I suspect my Alma may yet be secure from whim, and from
rival.

Infatuation, if not love, proves to be stronger than prudence; now Rychard in turn foolishly imagines himself to be worthy of Alma's amorous considerations. Jacques is forced to turn aside from his own meditations in the desert, where he has retired to await Alma's favor, in order to remind them all—Bouvard, Rychard, Alma, and himself—that everything grows from the seeds buried in one's own nature.

(Jacques Batârd to Rychard Artaud, October 1st, 2006)

>My mother is a withered crone,
>my father a professor,
>but both agree, a toad's a toad,
>and lower is the lesser.
>
>We spend our little lives
>running from our teachers,
>and after all our errantry
>come back to our own nature,
>
>where some, on deserts of the mind,
>waste their shriveled seed,
>and others father history
>in ogasms, and blood.
>
>Some were born for *eros*,
>some born to indecision;
>some were born for treachery,
>some born to be the hangman.

MANIFESTO OF THE NOVANAIVE

Homer went blind staring at the sun.
We smirk at the moon through our shades.

The sophisticate despises sentiment.
The ignorant despise irony.
The fearless vault over both.

Irony and sentimentality are two ends
of the same ass.

The animal expresses nature within.
Reason reflects nature without.
To become nature, we must make nature one.

Naivete is our end—
not the ignorant innocence of the child,
but the joy of the prodigal reclaiming Eden.

We have cheered, like drunken laggards, the post-enlightenment, the post-romantic, the post-victorian, the post-modern, the post-post-modern. Let us cast off our wineskins and tear down the goalposts!

THREE FANCIES

I was strolling my garden with William Blake, when I stopped to boast the novelty of my prize rose. The poet grimaced, sweating acid over a brow of copper: "Oh how these mills have ground to chaff the exhausted senses of your age! Where once the modest crimson of a wild bloom delighted bee and man alike, now a thousand artificial hues crowd for your shrunken desire." Reaching into the heart of the rose, he pulled out a tiny grub: "Monstrous arms, legs of iron, bowels belching blood and smoke, stumble over this tiny plot, and yet your eyes, your tongue, your ears, are as this invisible worm's, choked and dulled by your own excrement."

"I cannot see my heart," was my lament through a dark ale, while Sir Philip Sidney grinned at me through his carbuncles. "You are looking for a familiar word," he said, "but your heart is a strange muddle of clay and fire that you will scarcely recognize, and fear to own." "You are wrong," I sputtered, "that gelding, that pervert, that sophist, that dullard—it is not mine; and what is more, it does not exist!" "Let it speak." he assured me, "Everyone will swear that you have stolen their own tongue, and everyone will swear that they have never heard such golden words before."

I sat, with Dante, on the hills of the moon, our eyes on distant blue seas, while he swept an arc from Pole to Paradise. "From here," he sang, "it is all one chord. Everything changes, and everything is always the same; every circle is full, and every circle is necessary; and even the damned smile, behind their masks, at the reader's joy." Then, looking within, he blanched and saddened: "Below this sphere it is Guelf and Ghibelline, and what the blood hungers for here and now is not what the blood will hunger for there and then, and today's brief good must become law, and yesterday's laws must be broken."

A THICKET OF APHORISMS

To be original, by definition, is to be profoundly derivative.

Trains, radios, television, p.c.'s, ipods, feed our nostalgia. Bread and wine are always fresh.

The anarchist loves to be feared, but fears to be ignored.

Hail the nude, naked of politics!

You have seen nothing new, but your eyes are new.

Love truth more than the love of truth.

On this side—paradox, on the other—lobotomy.

The bison painted in smoke and ochre, the crosshatch scraped in the cavern wall—there are your schools of art!

The artist wants eternity now, and will work a lifetime to get it.

When sworn enemies forge an exhausted peace—that is tradition.

Paint is real. Photographs are imaginary.

Look in the mirror, once.

Every aphorism must be a lie.

Either the father devour the child, or the child devour the father.

For every god a hymn.

The black velvet puppy, the motel Elvis, are the beginnings of beauty.

When you tire of the funhouse, smash the mirrors.

I am invaded from within by self-replicating acids, from without by nomadic words. I am the city at the crossroads.

Long live the King—but not too long.

WHAT WE NEED NOW!
(SAN DIEGO, 2006)

Sobriety. Chastity. Fancy. Verse.

Gabriela Anaya Valdepeña: Beauty returns, without shame.

Delight in symmetry. Swallow chaos.

Olga Garcia: The Rape of Barbie.

If an image hides the naked thought, strip it off. If a thought pins the living image, pull it out.

Guy Lombardo: poop, plastic, politics.

This body. This wife. This house. This garden. This city.

Anna Zappoli: the bones in the tar pit.

Pentatonic Polyphony. The Cycladic Idol. Numbers.

Dan Adams: dog, light, oils, motion.

Paint your abstractions on the wall itself.

Chris Vannoy: The Cyborg's Progress.

The old self kills a new making. The new self makes the dead sing.

Richard Denner: wood, ink, word, vision.

Suburbs without satire.

David Bromige: nonsense, like speech.

Shadow. Space. Silence.

Paula Jones: Ezekiel's new bike.

There is room for the besotted bard, for the outraged child, for the self-consuming scholar, for the quilting bee—but not much room.

Attila Lukacs: history will never end.

And all the rest is "poetry."

www.ingramcontent.com/pod-product-compliance
Lightning Source LLC
Chambersburg PA
CBHW031955080426
42735CB00007B/402